The Voices

Books by Michael Dennis Browne:

The Wife of Winter (Rapp & Whiting, 1970)
The Wife of Winter (Charles Scribner, 1970)
Sun Exercises (Red Studio Press, 1976)
The Sun Fetcher (Carnegie Mellon, 1978)
Smoke from the Fires (Carnegie Mellon, 1985)
You Won't Remember This (Carnegie Mellon, 1992)
Selected Poems 1965-1995 (Carnegie Mellon, 1997)
Things I Can't Tell You (Carnegie Mellon, 2005)
Panthers (Indulgence Press, 2007)
What the Poem Wants (Carnegie Mellon, 2009)
The Voices (Carnegie Mellon, 2015)

The Voices

Michael Dennis Browne

CARNEGIE MELLON
UNIVERSITY PRESS

PITTSBURGH 2015

Acknowledgments

I am grateful to the editors of the following publications and organizations with whom some of these words first appeared: American Public Media, BIS Records, Enskyment, Lost Hills Press, Indulgence Press, Paulus Publications, Reformed Worship, G. Schirmer, *Spirituality Today*, DownStairs Press, Yarroway Mountain Press, *Great River Review, Bearings, Tinderbox Poetry Journal, Sleet*.

I am very grateful for support from the Graduate School of the University of Minnesota, the Fesler-Lampert Endowment, Brush Creek Foundation for the Arts, Collegeville Institute of Cultural and Ecumenical Research, Basilica of Saint Mary (Minneapolis), The MacDowell Colony.

Special thanks to David Bengtson, Jim Moore, Ken McCullough, Peter McLean-Browne. And always to Cynthia Lamb and Gerald Costanzo, my editors.

To Be Certain of the Dawn is available as a CD from BIS Records. "For the Young Men to Sing" is published as "We Are" by G. Schirmer. A recording of "Seven Last Voices" is on American Public Media (Performance Today). *Panthers,* a limited edition fine press book, is available as a free PDF download from Indulgence Press.

Cover photo by Dave Schwarz, used with the permission of *St. Cloud Times* and Times Media. The photograph is of students from three Minnesota college choirs approaching the gates of a former concentration camp in France, where they performed the post-Holocaust oratorio *To Be Certain of the Dawn*.

Website: michaeldennisbrowne.com

Library of Congress Control Number 2014943697
ISBN 978-0-88748-594-7
Copyright © 2015 by Michael Dennis Browne
All rights reserved
Book design by Matt Finlay
Printed and bound in the United States of America
10 9 8 7 6 5 4 3 2 1

for Stephen Paulus

Contents

1

The Voices 13
Seven Last Voices 15

    1 / HOUSE 15
    2 / THIEF 17
    3 / MOTHER 19
    4 / TSUNAMI 21
    5 / LINE 23
    6 / OVER 24
    7 / PANTOKRATOR 26

2

To Be Certain of the Dawn 31

    CREATE IN ME 31
    KINGDOM OF NIGHT 33
    TWO LITTLE GIRLS 35
    OLD MAN, YOUNG MAN 37
    THREE COATS 39
    BOY READING 41
    HYMN OF THE ETERNAL FLAME 43
    WALKING WITH YOU 44
    VOICES OF SURVIVORS 46

The Unfolding: a Ruah Prayer 47
The Road Home 49
August Hymn 50
For the Young Men to Sing 51
Song of Gratitude 53
Carol of the Stranger 55

3

Shorts	59
Wash Wish	73
Words	74
The Children	75
Kin	76
Flags on Their Poles	77
Brother Dream	78
Blind	79
Aftershock	80
After Lorca	81
After Anna Swir, Again	82

4

In Memory of Chester Anderson	85
The Old Man and the Poem	87
October Prayer	88
Dietrich in the Pure Land	89
Shall We Gather	90
Students on the Edge	91
Catalpa	93
My Rain	94
Even in This Rain	95
Fire	100
For Kilian at Ninety	101
Midnight	102
Emergency Room, Mount Sinai, New York City	103
For George McGovern	104
The Old Happiness	105
Melody	106
"wanted to be an artist"	107
For the Wedding of Mary and Marc	108

The mingling of both well-being and distress in us is so astonishing that we can hardly tell what state we are in. But the fact is, that is part of being whole. We stand in this mingling all our lives.

—Julian of Norwich

I

The Voices

for Dale Warland and the singers
on the occasion of their farewell concert,
May 30, 2004

I don't know if we have ever deserved
    the voices, but they are ours,
I don't know if we ever have known
    what it means to be able to speak
in those tongues, and only
    in my worst, most useless moments
have I tried to imagine
    our lives without them.
Where might we go in the world
    where they would not reach us?

I would never go into the dark
    without the voices,
I have come to rely on how they mend us
    among the ruins
of what we have hoped for.
    If there were only one branch in the world,
the voices would find it.

Doubt was never the root of us,
    doubt winds itself, again and again,
around our doing,
    but it was never the source,

joy is the source,
    foliage of joy in which
the singers are hidden, but heard;
    always the gate, always the garden,
always the light, the shadows,
    always the leaves.

From where I stand now,
    I cannot see every singer,
but looking out across the years,
    listening in ways learned
only from them,
    I can hear all the song.

Seven Last Voices

in response to
The Seven Last Words of Our Savior on the Cross
by Franz Josef Haydn

I / HOUSE

"Father, forgive them, for they know not what they do"
"Pater, dimitte illis; non enim sciunt quid faciunt"

You are descending stairs—
    down and down and down.
Slowly, as in dream.
    You have never wanted to go this deep,
but the House of Forgiveness is large.

As if you were among the roots of oaks.
    Up there, storms;
you know the branches grind and shriek,
    but here no groaning, only this quietness,
as of whales asleep.

Is this down here the dream?
    Or is it up there, where you do
things as wild as, wilder than,
    those plunging branches?

All hates, little and large, that you hold,
    let those winds sweep them from you,

send them as leaves down the street,
    let *these* deeps murmur to you,
wary of them as you were
    (and now their salt
washing your wounds clean).

Forgiveness—has she lived here all along?
    Out of her blood once you came,
and so soon you hissed away from her,
    from whose body you began by drinking
before you learned any words
    to distance yourself from her.

And why such a stranger here?
    Why have you lived away?
Why only a guest in these rooms?
    Descending now, breathing this darker air;
what is to be done
    other than watch and listen
out of the heart she gave you?

Now windows are being opened,
    you feel it everywhere,
and what is this fragrance
    all through the air?
It is forgiveness.
    Forgiveness and her flowers.

2 / THIEF

"This day you will be with me in paradise"
"Hodie mecum eris in paradiso"

At least they did not cut off my hands
    and leave me helpless.
At least they have only killed me,

Where you go, now I go.
    You said: come with me,
you shall be with me.
    You said: I know the paths.
So: I will follow you.

All I know is that we die
    here together.
All I can do is trust you,
    tied as I am beside you.

My own crimes, I know.
    Too many, too often.
What was yours?
    Was there the one only?
A large one?
    (They seem to have made
larger wounds in you.)

At dawn light this morning—
    it was so cold, remember?—
I did not know that now
    I would be walking these paths with you.
Are we near water?
    I think I see boats,
hear what sounds like ropes,
    slapping against masts
within a harbor.

This going with you,
    I already love.

As a boy,
    I never knew the names of trees,
but these are cedars.

3 / MOTHER

"Woman, behold your son"
"Mulier, ecce filius tuus"

I thought I *had* my son in this life.
    And now, you give me another.

When did you ever not surprise me?
    It was not always an amazement I would have chosen,
but each time, like a dream, it was there
    and I belonged to it.

Do I hold *this* one to my heart?
    Is that what I must do?

As if forgiveness were not already enough,
    already so much,
now this?

Was there ever a time you did not ask of me
    more than I thought I could do?
I have never dreamed myself as large
    as you presume me to be.
Really, there are only so many rooms.

You never let me live my only life;
    you never did.

But in all you have asked of me,
    I did not fail you and I will not now,
even now, though this is hardest,
    here in this place where you suffer so.

When I said yes—so long ago—
    to be your mother—
I was young, young—
    how could I have known
what this would ask of me?
    And could this be the last asking,
as you die before me?

I hardly think so.

I never knew how much
    could break in me,
and still be green.

And now you say, my son:
    Behold your son.
You cannot ask it, and you do.

Here I am.

4 / TSUNAMI

"My God, My God, why have You abandoned me?
"Eli, Eli, lamma sabacthani?"

The sea has taken everything. What has the sea *not* taken?

The sun looks like a scar, the birds like scars in the branches—
where there is any kind of tree.

Why is there nothing? (The something, as it just was, was never so
much.)
Why is there now nothing?

Why is there another day after this one? Then another, then another?

What are the nights for? Yet I prefer the sky dark, so I never
expect a sun.
I prefer the poor light of stars.

Dark, or light, there is nothing left to dream.

My God, My God, I cannot begin to ask what You were thinking.
I cannot begin to dare to imagine that You might have turned away
just a moment from the world, even that You were beginning
to think of a different world, wearying of this one . . .

I cannot believe that for even a moment You drew back Your heart
from us.
Why, then, *this heartlessness?*

We have been betrayed not only by the sea, but especially
the sea. Everything we had broken; everything known.

Lord, You, even You, even if You are there in some lost corner
of my heart, calling like a mad bird, I do not hear You. Instead
I call and call.

Am I still Your bird, even if I am a mad one?

My God, My God, I always knew You were with us.
Now do I know?

Mother, mother of my mother, mothers, can you tell me
anything beyond my own question with its thousand mouths:
Why?

When I was a child, always they told me there was light,
that the light was real, but was hidden. And now?

Hidden is beating its drum, its drum, its drum.

5 / LINE

"I thirst"
"Sitio"

I do not know how long the line is. I know I am not the first of the thirsty, not the last. The line goes round the world.

Cracked the lips of the children; the lips of the mothers, the lips of the fathers.

The belly is a begging bowl, a shallow little thing. It trembles, but we are not to see that. (Only surgeons, like ravens high above the body, could look down and in.)

These are lives in which rain has not fallen for years: no slow steady soaking of rain in the night, no loosened earth, no fragrance, no flowers unfolding, no silky lotus with its leaves unfurled.

Lord, now that we know You thirst, what is our own dryness but Yours? Yours but ours? You thirst, since You are with us, even till the end of time, Your bowl no bigger. With us in this line.

Did you tremble in Your own abandonment? I have imagined Your wounds so wide that small animals ran there to hide from the hunters—nothing You could do about it, nothing You would have chosen to do, even if Your hands had not been nailed to wood.

No creature too small for You to be its savior, to take upon Yourself its thirst.

The line goes round the world. Your world.

6 / OVER

"It is finished"
"Consummatum est"

Apples. Olives. Table. Door. Dust. Rain.

It is over.

The whale in her deeps. The hawk, circling.

Scar. Cut. Bruise. Vein. Pulse. Bone.

Over.

Mud. Straw. Coins. Dawn. Twigs. Wind.

Your mother's songs. Your father's stories. Games with the little friends.

Over.

The sheep with their bells. The goats—of course the goats.

Hands. Lips. Bread. Fingers. Tears. Healing.

It is over. Pockets emptied of minutes and hours and days.

Mercy, the oil.
Mercy, the womb.
Mercy, the breath.

Over.

Now go to Mercy herself.
The One who always strengthened You.
The One in whom there was nothing You could not do.

Waves rolling onto the shore, sliding away.

It is over. It begins.
It is over. It begins.

Riddles. Blessings. Teachings. Streams. Leaves. Birds.
(Maybe the birds go with You.)

Now, how can we not know what must die in us?
What must grow less?
What lives?

It is over. It begins.
It is over. It begins.

It is over. It begins.

7 / PANTOKRATOR

"Father, into Your hands I let go my spirit"
"In manus tuas, Domine, commendo spiritum meum"

What did not begin with You?

What goes back to You has always been with You—
    in Your hands, we say, but *not that, not that,*
        we know You are Spirit, that there are no hands,
          and when were we ever not in them?

How do we return to You?
    Ground of our being (*not that, not that*),
        Ruler of All (*not that, not that*)
          though *Father*, we can say, though *Mother*,
            since from the first breath
              we have loved those names.

In our need, in our joy, we have spoken to You,
    little intimate conversations,
        Who knew us since before we were born.
          Nothing we would not say to You
            Who know all the rivers we are.
              Nothing in us that does not flow to You.

Into Your hands, though Your hands are the sky,
    into Your heart, though Your heart is all flowers . . .
        See, we cannot imagine You!
          And *since* we cannot imagine You—
            Immensity, forgive us, then.

With what does not die,
    with what in us does not know how to die,
      we come.
        Like children,
          like leaves before the wind.
            Father. Mother. To You.

2

from the oratorio
To Be Certain of the Dawn

This is the task: in the darkest night to be certain of the dawn, certain of the power to turn a curse into a blessing, agony into a song. To know the monster's rage and, in spite of it, proclaim to its face (even a monster will be transfigured into an angel); to go through Hell and to continue to trust in the goodness of God—this is the challenge and the way.
—Abraham Joshua Heschel

You must teach the children, so they can remake the world.
—Abraham Joshua Heschel

CREATE IN ME
(*Chorus*)

Create a great emptiness in me.
Send a wind.
Lay bare the branches.
Strip me of usual song.
Drop me like a stone,
so that I go
where a stone goes.
Send me down unknown paths,
send me into pathlessness.
into the lost places,
down into echoes

to where I hear
voices, but no words:
a place of weeping
below any of earth's waters.

    Teshuvah
        Teshuvah
            Teshuvah

Give me difficult dreams
where my skills
will not serve me.
Make bitter the wines
I have stored.

Begin the returning.

    Teshuvah
        Teshuvah
            Teshuvah

KINGDOM OF NIGHT
(Chorus)

Holy God, who find no strength in us
    to be Your power.
How should we think ourselves
    Your hands, Your feet?
How should we be Your heart?

On the day You called to us,
    in the kingdom of night
where You kept calling,
    how did we heal one another
in Your name? How did we think
    we might be recognized as You
in all we failed to do?
    In the kingdom of night
where, again and again,
    out of the mouths of children,
You kept calling.

Where was the light
    we should have been?
Moons we are, ghosts we were;
    no way for anyone to know
that great sun shone.

And everywhere such wounds.

This we ask of You—
    You who brought us into being—
which tasks are ours? which labors?
    which joys? which dances?
which instruments of Yours
    do we become?

In the time of the breaking of glass,
    the tearing of roots,
the splitting of every little temple
    of hope, the heart,
breathe in us, Spirit of God,
    so that we strengthen,
so we may grow and be known
    by our love.

TWO LITTLE GIRLS
(*Soprano, Mezzo-Soprano*)

two little girls
we are just two little girls
in the street

sisters?
what do you think?

maybe so
maybe not
maybe so

we're a little bit curious about the camera
we're not so unhappy about the camera

(who is it,
we wonder,
who is looking at us
just the two of us)

here we are

do you like the skirt?
what do you think of the coat?
pretty red coat!
it's Tuesday
so I get the coat for the day
Leah is wearing the skirt

why bread
in both my hands?
why does Leah
have nothing at all?

she has one hand
on the back of my neck
she's holding onto me
the other hand's empty

just in case
just in case

hands are for holding onto
hands are never for hurting us
hands are for giving us things

what do you think of our shoes???

OLD MAN, YOUNG MAN
(Baritone)

you can keep standing there
if you want

I'm going to stay
sitting here with my back
against this tree
and smiling to see you
just being so young

(maybe it's something
you're saying to me
I don't remember)

maybe it's because
I am father
to your mother

maybe that's not really
a smile on my face
maybe I'm half-asleep
and I'm having a dream
where I'm leaning against a tree
and Rachel's boy is standing
slender in sunlight
talking with me

I want this dream
to go on and on
and things are still good
or good enough
in this world of summer

and nothing so bad
has happened to us
not under these trees
where you stand
your back to the camera
young child of a man
young child of my child
talking with me

as if you were made of sunlight
as if you were made of leaves

THREE COATS
(*Mezzo-Soprano, Tenor*)

I'm wearing three coats
or maybe it's
two jackets and a coat

I have curls hidden under
my knitted cap
am I a girl or a boy?
it doesn't matter!

(a girl)

under the coats
there's a shirt,
it's buttoned-up, too

(a boy)

and I'm wearing
a scarf
between my shirt and my vest

I just wish
it didn't hurt
where my tooth came out
didn't look so bad

and if only I wasn't
so sleepy today
(bad dreams)

and if only
father didn't look
so scared last night
when we heard
the knocking on the door

so—

a shirt
a scarf
a vest
a jacket
a coat

(I'm a boy!)
(I'm a bundled-up boy!)

BOY READING
(*Baritone*)

I'm looking down
from far away
I'm high up on a branch
looking down
on the book

so many little characters
all of them keys,
says Mama,
keys to all the doors
I want to open

keys
doors
I want to open them all

I like the way
the characters are
sometimes I think I see
looks on their faces
(*they're* looking at *me*)

they'll take me
into the stories
where I want to go

I had a dream
where I grew so heavy
I fell out of the tree
down down down
into the characters

and they covered me over
and no one could find me

they never found me

HYMN OF THE ETERNAL FLAME
(Children's Chorus, Soprano)

Every face is in you,
    Every voice,
Every sorrow in you,
    Every pity,
Every love, every memory,
    Woven into fire.

Every breath is in you,
    Every cry,
Every longing in you,
    Every singing,
Every hope, every healing,
    Woven into fire.

Every heart is in you,
    Every tongue,
Every trembling in you,
    Every blessing,
Every soul, every shining,
    Woven into fire.

WALKING WITH YOU
(*Soprano, Baritone, Tenor, Mezzo-Soprano*)

I would like to be walking with you.
in the cool of the evening.

Walking with you
in the streets of that city
we have imagined and dreamed.

There we are walking.

Not evening, maybe. Maybe in the heat of noon.
Or midnight with its winds.
Not a time of our choosing.

Do not fear, I am with you.
I will bring your offspring from the east
and from the west I will gather you.
I will say to the north, "Give them up,"
and to the south, "Do not withhold;
bring My sons from far away
and My daughters from the end of the earth."

Maybe a rain
running down the leaves,
running over the stones,
down the roots of the trees

We are walking there.

Source of All Life,
 these eyes and faces
are You among us
 as we labor to repair this world.

Maybe stars,
 those faithful ones
that do not step down;
 we will walk by their light,
and ask forgiveness
 for smallness of dreams.

I would like to be walking with you
 in the cool of the evening;
I would like to be walking
 in the streets of that city
we have dreamed and imagined;
 there we are walking.

music by Stephen Paulus

VOICES OF SURVIVORS
(Soprano, Tenor, Baritone, Mezzo-Soprano)

"I see the places, the people—they live in my memory—the faces of the people who meant so much to me."
(Felicia Weingarten, survivor)

"Why did I survive? The Rabbi said: 'God kept you on earth to write the story.'"
(Henry Oertelt, survivor; zl, of blessed memory)

"I dream of the sculpture of a bird—I try to touch it. I wake up touching the bird. I think it is a miracle."
(Robert Fisch, survivor)

"I have lived in a world with no children. . . . I would never live in a world of no children again."
(Hinda Kibort, survivor; zl; of blessed memory)

music by Stephen Paulus

This work was commissioned by the Basilica of Saint Mary in Minneapolis as an offering of the Christian community to the Jewish community on the occasion of the fortieth anniversary of the Vatican document Nostra Aetate *and the sixtieth anniversary of the liberation of the death camps.*

The Unfolding: a Ruah Prayer
(for women's voices)

When were You ever not
    our Mother?
When were Your wings ever not
    in us?

O Thou   *O Thou*
     Ruah   *Ruah*

As once You moved over the face
    of the waters,
even so we feel Your flowing,
    Your flowing through us.

     Ruah   *Ruah*

Our sister You are,
    our Always,
our Neverendingness.
    As wheat gleaming, so we
should dream.

O Thou   *O Thou*   *O Thou*
     Ruah   *Ruah*   *Ruah*

In the night You are with us,
    nearer than near.
How should we fear?
    You will not let the heart
be lost, be lost, be lost
    in the shadows.

O Thou	*O Thou*	*O Thou*
Ruah	*Ruah*	*Ruah*

With every folding, unfolding,
    folding, unfolding,
all waves of the world,
    all worlds of Your making
within us, revealed.

O Thou	*O Thou*	*O Thou*
Veni	*Veni*	
O Thou	*O Thou*	*O Thou*
Holy	*Healing*	
Ruah	*Ruah*	*Ruah*
Veni	*Veni*	
O Thou	*O Thou*	*O Thou*

in memory of my sisters

music by Donald Krubsack

The Road Home

Tell me where is the road
    I can call my own,
That I left, that I lost,
    So long ago?
All the years I have wandered,
    Oh when will I know
There's a way, there's a road
    That will lead me home?

After wind, after rain,
    When the dark is done,
As I wake from a dream
    In the gold of day
Through the air there's a calling
    From far away,
There's a voice I can hear
    That will lead me home.

Rise up, follow me,
    Come away, is the call,
With the love in your heart
    As the only song;
There is no such beauty
    As where you belong;
Rise up, follow me,
    I will lead you home.

new arrangement by Stephen Paulus of a melody
from the Southern Harmony Songbook, *1835*

August Hymn

We do not tire of dreams you bring,
    Of ageless rumors often told,
Or all these years of love for you,
    Your tales, your parables.

We kneel amid your harvest gold.
    We see your stillness in the day,
We feel your tremblings in the dark,
    Your leaves, your mysteries.

We bow before your silences,
    We know that they have heard before
What we are murmuring to them,
    Your stars, your dragonflies.

We want no other earth than this,
    This everywhere of holiness,
While all about the kingdom sway
    Your rains, your promises.

For the Young Men to Sing

for Peter McLean-Browne

we are all sons of fathers and mothers
we are all sons

singing

we are all rivers
the roar of waters

what is the world to us?
who can we be for the world?

there is a star at morning and one at evening
they are no more the names we give them
than we are

everything singing beyond itself
beyond the names we love (O Love) to give them

everything swelling beyond its powers
everything lifted up in the singing

we are sparks that scatter through the world
from original fire we come

we are the flow of sky and its unfolding
we are hundreds of hoofbeats on hard ground

sometimes no home for us on the earth
no place to lay our heads

if you could know for one moment
how it is to stand in our bodies
within the world

you ask too much of us
you ask too little

everything brimming in us
everything dark in its barrel

we are
          be
we are
              become
we are
                  bless
we are
                      dream

we are all sons

singing

music by Craig Hella Johnson

Song of Gratitude

Out of this love, out of this longing,
    Out of these voices from all of the ages,
Out of these songs, out of this singing,
    Lifting our souls, lifting our being:
Heart, you are everywhere,
    Deeper than dreaming;
In the name of the spirit of love,
    Always and everywhere,
We bow down, we bow down:
    Namaste.

Within the source, within the center,
    Within the telling of falling and rising,
Within the root, within creation,
    Harvest of waves, dancing redeeming:
Hope, you flow everywhere,
    Healing our hunger;
In the name of the spirit of love,
    Always and everywhere,
We bow down, we bow down:
    Namaste

Harmony flesh, harmony treasure,
    Harmony human, forever returning,
Harmony path, harmony vision,
    Blessing our way, endless beginnings:
Light, you shine everywhere,
    Shaping our wonder;

In the name of the spirit of love,
    Always and everywhere,
We bow down, we bow down:
    Namaste.

music by Craig Hella Johnson

Carol of the Stranger

Peace and grace be to this house
　　Where all are welcomed in;
Receive the guest, receive this heart:
　　Tell the Stranger, tell.

　　Tell the Stranger what you cannot tell
　　Those who love you and desire your joy:
　　Tell.

Make tall your walls, make long these beams,
　　Who once believed alone;
Make wide the circle, feed the fire:
　　Tell the Silence, tell.

　　Tell the Silence what you cannot tell
　　Those who love you and desire your joy.
　　Tell.

Blessings be upon this place,
　　Let every wound be healed,
Every secret, every dream:
　　Tell the Angel, tell.

　　Tell the Angel what you cannot tell
　　Those who love you and desire your joy.
　　Tell.

Peace and grace be to this house,
    All will be returned;
Let every soul be called your own,
    Tell the Mystery, tell.

    Tell the Mystery what you cannot tell
    Those who love you and desire your joy.
    Tell.

music by Abbie Betinis

3

Shorts

AFTER ANNA SWIR

old pearl with no shine
old shine of the subtle secret

old brain of pearl
old pearl Bible of the one page

pearl infant asleep
pearl dog dreaming

pearly scripture gleaming
impenetrable pearl masterpiece

YOUR HAIR

I love your hair.
I love how your hair
shines. I love how your hair
rows
across the Atlantic.

AT THE CONVENT

I dance with my pearly Dad
I dance with my auntie the nun

I eat the awful sandwiches

BEACH

I was on a beach
I was a wild stone

the wind blew me all
about the world

though I was stone

MY ELEGY

I'll take just a short one, please
maybe a form
of some kind
maybe summat wi' rhyme

or else words
wild, unleashed and free
as verse
is said to be

BEATER

your Dad drives some old car
I seen him

your Dad's old, too
I seen the rust on him

got a convertible head
know what I mean?

yeah I seen
the rust on him

INVITATION

I've been invited
to the White House

to a ceremony
in the rose garden

to receive a medal
for anxiety

I'm not going

RIVER

one day the midwife
    bent over and was busy

and then my river
    of a boy began

BROTHER DREAM

walking with you slowly
over the trembling green

our feet seeming to float
as once they used to

my satchel heavy
with old coins

your face in profile
on one side

mine on the other

FOREST OF DEAN

our mother walks
        into the trees
until we see her
        no more

we follow, walk
        where she walked
bend to touch
        the flowers

she grows
        as she goes

CALL

once a day call yourself up
that huge laugh others hear
coming at you from yourself
you hearing you laughing

FOX

I'm so sleepy, I say to the fox
feel as if I'm walking in my sleep

is there something wrong with us?

ELEGY FOR THE WORLD

the sun always rose
till now—
and the moon—O Mother,
what she did to the sky!

and the birds
their flying done
just lean out giddy
over the highest branch

and look down

IVORY-BILLED WOODPECKER

return of the legendary
Lord God Bird

you who will
one day

wipe away
all tears

DAD

his keyboards, his fast fingers
his feet in dancing pumps on the pedals

the schooner Toccata
the sloop Fugue

deer running through the church

DIRT ROAD

I like to talk dirt to the road
I have a mucky mouth filled with gaps
I have mud for a dog
and a broken leash understanding

HORSES

keep hearing them
along the river

making the leaves crack
making the coins spin

in the streets
of the city of horses

where it is always
raining or grieving

MY SISTER HOLDING HER HAT IN A HIGH WIND

not Angela actually
in America

somebody's sister

on a street corner
where I am being made

mad by wind

EMPTY NEST

the birds have flown
how great to be
here on our own
(this sun, this moon)

DOG AND THE RAIN

dog barks at the rain

dog says to the rain, you want to come over
to my place for some fun?

dog says, you want to go to the park
and run circles with me?

meet you there, rain?

dog would go to a movie with rain
if rain were allowed in

DOGS

I remember I have forgotten
our old dogs,

like a prayer
I have been too lazy to say

now once again
here they are

running along
in the dark

SMALL HOURS

Is that dust on your sleep or gold?
Is that sleep on your eyes or dust?
Is that flesh on your arm or bone?

QUEENS

several of the queens of England
hide in me

in fear
for their barren lives

several of Henry's queens,
trembling

ELECTION DAY MORNING

as many voters
    in lines
        as yellow leaves

all of us
    somehow
        fallen

READING SOMEONE'S MSS.

as if am diving from a high board
lose my hands on the way down

wondering how to make
the neatest incision without them

even as I enter

PANTHERS

seen
    running
        among
            the
                meanings

FLYCATCHER

I can't think of anything
    to tell the flycatcher
        to do differently

I wish I knew how to twitch
    my tail right there
        in the center

of a bare dead branch
    and look
        so meant-to-be.

JAZZ BANDAGE

dusk
    as the words
        begin their slide

and the evening
    of meaning
        is here

MARY MY SISTER

help Mary in drowned heaven
our safe little remember stream children
cloud watercress shadow buttercup cattle long grass
farm sky tremble willow oak leaning
your crown of wet thorns

MIDNIGHT

All England comes back to me.
Have not forgotten
a gate, a field, a lane.
All childhood seasides are there.

For the head on the pillow,
all hours
are visiting hours.

INCISION

one half Iraq
one half Tsunami

nor think they
will ever close

MAY

even in the hostile
    neighbor's yard,
        blossom

DREAM

ring rolled toward a drain
but a finger

reached out of the drain
and the ring fit fine

THE SUN GOES

down
on our street
and in the dark
the red
buildings
shimmer

SON

and you were so happy
when the director in my Danish nightmare
said "call me in the morning"

because although you'd likely be cast
as merely a handsome demon
(the only kind of movie they make)

you had a part

YOU

you with a canoe
for a head—
don't paddle your child
backwards!

TO YOU

Now I look long into your eyes,
as I have never done before.
Eyes brown as an owl's wing.
I see avenues, avenues.
We should go walking there.

STILL WONDERING

which parts
of the dark

are not meant
to be mended

UP NORTH

in bed in the woods
        in the afternoon
I get up to go
        look for a friend

whose singing
        I think I hear
from a rooftop
        in a tough part of town

by the time I'm dressed
        get out into green
the song has ended

WHAT WAS SAID WHEN THE BROTHERS AND SISTERS WERE IN THE SAME ROOM TOGETHER FOR THE FIRST TIME IN TEN YEARS

if this was a hundred years ago
we would all have lived in the same village
we would have been able to help one another
we would have seen one another all the time

June 2 (Thomas Hardy's birthday)

Wash Wish

what the tree means when
there's a grief in the air

wash wish

by the tree I mean the pine
by the pine I mean the moan

wash wish

when the leaves when some
saying of wind to be done

wash wish

by the leaves I mean the needles
by the needles I mean the pain

wash wish

when the need when some
swaying of pain to be sung

Words

some died on their way to you
some had a child by you
and you never knew

some come by in the night
and, finding the fool asleep,
move on

some speak in a thick tongue
some in delighted
lovers' cries

some on the same
bus as you

some on watch
from skinny trees
at the edge of town

The Children

the children come into the dream
because there are so many roads

in pairs, in threes
or one who is alone

they do not say *it should have been*
they say *it is so* and *it is so*

we cannot keep them
from leaving

on to the next dream and the next
and the next

worn coats and pants
and shirts and shoes

no bread, no soup
for the journey

on to the next dream
and the next and the next

it is so

Kin

you are all my kin

in the small hours
I claim you

set out in your shadow boats
let us meet

arriving
by sail, by paddle, by oar

on a vastness of water
however wild it may be

all of you my kin
and I claim you

Flags on Their Poles

like beasts in their stalls
shifting

but no one
is coming

to milk them
or rub them down

just over
and over

the lowering
the raising

the only life
they know

Brother Dream

in which he is playing cards
on the lawn with Prokofiev

(to whom I have been listening)
in England, in the English countryside,

(which I happen to be visiting)
only now he is Wilfred Owen

(about whom I have been reading)
though I am the one who died young

with our father's smile on my face,
soaked in a trench with flowers

woven by snipers into white rumors
(to which I have been contributing),

both of us borne in full uniform
round and round a nightclub

down a dank alley named
The Birds of Paradise.

Blind

you do not steer on this
wide river

the captain is not
asleep at the wheel

is blind and is
your captain

no one on board
complains

he being
the most

recommended
of guides

such a captain

Aftershock

the blind god
does not know

why he is
being led

to the firing
squad

why they have
bothered to bind him

why everything goes
so reluctantly

or what he did
wrong with the world

After Lorca

there was nothing in there
    you could have wanted
only an empty room
    with three horses in it

there was nothing in there
    you could have taken

only a painting on the wall
    sealed to the wall
with the blood
    of some creature

only the portrait
    of an owl staring out
from the eyeball
    of a horse

there was nothing
    inside the page
nothing inside the ink
    that did not echo

nothing with wings
    nothing with reliable sorrow

After Anna Swir, Again

steered as I slept
dreaming of Angela

my sister near

last night began
the book

Freeing the Soul from Fear

fell asleep reading
almost rear-ending

a blue car
wet with white

blossoms of alphabet

meaningless vehicle
of the kind

I dream of driving

4

In Memory of Chester Anderson

You have stopped breathing, but I read the poem
to its end: "Their eyes, their ancient glittering eyes, are gay."
No more breastbone. Your fifty states cease. Nor shining sea.

These days, weeks later, I am wearing your clothes.
I wore them round Ireland, I wear them here in Iowa,
this city where you trained in wartime. It is wartime again.
Sometimes I think I see you on the street,
here where my life began again. For sure
I glimpse you down the lanes of tunes.

How come, a dozen days ago, I got to hear Seamus
reading in Dublin or, days before that, in far Belmullet,
Thomas Kinsella? Though, had you been there, how much
would you have heard? How much seen?
And how long might it have taken you
to journey there, to stony Mayo?

They took your eyes for research. Nobody asked,
as far as I know, for your ears, that had become
almost as little use to you. Nobody
could commandeer, Old Pal, your voices
or your voice. Who better rowed the boat of words
than you? More kindled the syllables, Jaysus, man,
more held them up to the light?
Jeweler, you.

"For Fergus rules the brazen cars
And rules the shadows of the wood,
And the white breast of the dim sea
And all disheveled wandering stars."

They can have my heart one day, if they want it.
They can have any part of me.

Chester Anderson 1923-2006

The Old Man and the Poem

you are the old man and the poem
you are the old poem who went on
beyond the words beyond the breath
(little wishbone of a breastbone
ceasing its negligible motion)

I am who kept saying
the words to you who went on
into the no breath beyond
the poem's breathing and your friend

who wear now what you wore
now wrap your robe around me
as wind rattles windows
easily rattled the window and the reader

but never your beyond of breath
nor ever the saying the singing
that so long ago once
we were dreamed into being

Chester Anderson 1923-2006

October Prayer

for Dietrich Reinhart OSB

When it seems there is so
  much to be done,

and how little there is I can do,

I calm to become
  the cottonwood's wrinkled bark

and not the millions of crows

I once would have been,
  straining their raw voices

so high in the tree of life.

Help me, help me again,
  my only God.

Dietrich in the Pure Land

How cold that pine box must quickly have become.
We had stepped forward to spill dark earth onto the lid.
I slept poorly that night within sight of the cemetery.
The animated man is gone,
there is no seeing him,
there is only the doing to be done of the ways he followed,
his vision to be carried on.
That box holds no living water.
The River Dietrich flows on in an elsewhere of fire.

Shall We Gather

where twisted lengths of girders
    lie along the riverbank
they seem like scraps of sky
    that dropped, dragging
its birds with them

and these were people,
    unknown, loved,
who flew awhile
    (as everyone dreams to do)
in this world of falling

Highway 35 bridge
August 2007, Minneapolis

Students on the Edge

we sang
over, oh over
the thorn
    —Paul Celan

I'm sorry we had to bring you here
    —Rabbi Joseph Edelheit

As though you do not want to leave, arms around one another,
black-gowned, black-suited, standing above the bruising valley.

Silence with her fingers on your shoulders.

Nothing in you soars above this rupture. No wing lifts this grief.

But you made your music here, sang into the Pit, vile cold
rooms with their stains and drains, wept in the silence after the
last note.

No; bless. Heal. *Tikkun.*

Birds' wordless songs. Trees bleed shadow. No pine speaks.

It has given you a number, this valley. Yours to wear. It walks
behind you—see, it follows.

Sometimes it seems we might need to forgive God for . . . for . . .
but we keep forgetting. Forgetting our blaming, our God.

Be awake. Bless. Be awake in the world.

*for the Minnesota musicians after their oratorio
performance at Natzweiler Struthof Concentration Camp,
Alsace-Lorraine, France*

Catalpa

for Joe Sodd, dancer, murdered, June 22, 2008

There they are at last,
    the white blossoms
always arriving mid-June,
    after lilac, after more obvious
and beautiful blossoms are done;
    we should keep faith, Catalpa.

But you, young flower of a man,
    where do we look for *you?*
Where is our help now
    in this sudden winter?
Where are you to be found?
    What might you say to us?

In the heart, friends,
    these first hours of summer,
their silky winds, their blossoms,
    little bells shaking that do not ring;
remember, remember,
    only there.

From this darkness, these shadows,
    hoping, hoping,
never forgetting,
    and we will need a guide
to lead us to where
    forever you are.

Show us, show us, Joe.

My Rain

I heard you last night

My wife went out in you to give our son's friend a ride home
I wondered, if she were never to return, could I ever forgive you?

I didn't know you were still that strong

I love seeing the young, the waves and waves of them
I forget that the sky is young

I don't envy the young
I love them as I love the rain

The rain that also bewilders me
The exhausting rain

Sometimes I feel like dry old grass

Then comes my rain

Even in This Rain

in memory of Matthew Shepard

"When there are so many we shall have to mourn" —W. H. Auden

how could we say to you
we have ceased to dream

(to imagine, to praise)

you need us to be dreaming

whoever we are to become
we owe you our grief
our joy

and you want us to go on

even in this rain

2

standing in these bare spaces
in this wind, shaking

wind-herds swarming

twigs, branches, leaves
being torn away

into worlds where we cannot follow

thunder stamping where it wants
lightning's wires loose and writhing

and you want us to go on
not to lose our desire

even in this rain

3

our breathing must seem a music to you
we the living

moment by moment
this majesty
of breath and being

every breath
remembers

whoever you might want us
to become

you need us to be dreaming
(must dream, must dream)

there is no forgetting

even in this rain

4

no revenge

the thunder is not from you
the lightning not your agony

no forgetting

and you want us to hold
what we tremble to hold

you need us not to let go
even in this rain
this wind
          wind
                    wind
these storms

everything soaked
muddy

and the blood
our dreaming
you need our dreaming

no revenge
no forgetting

even in this rain

5

among these grasses swaying
beside these cottonwoods

wandering the banks of these racing rivers

crows calling, calling
(nothing we can know)

no, not our despair
those cracked wheels creaking

as if you might say
(voice that is walking on the falling sky)

I want you to go on
you want us to go on

I need you to dream

you need us to dream
even in this rain

6

our day be new to us
        each one, each dawn
world where you are not
        from which
we speak to you

Matthew, Matthew

and you persisting
        in your silence of speaking to us
in this darkness
        even in this rain

or yes, on any starry night

whose far
        whose near
                whose trembling
fires
        always
                you are

Fire

An old woman brought you to us,
    first on her back, then dragged
across snow the last miles.
    Crows scraped around her
with their sour cries.

Her boys not there to help,
    never heard from since soldiers
took them, and her daughter still
    in the dark room
where the soldiers left her.

Curled on the earth, she dreamed
    a tall ship
sliding into harbor with this burden,
    but when she woke, early,
the wood lay heaped before her.

I would put coins in her hands,
    at least try to warm them,
but she is gone already,
    vanished into the next place, the next,
leaving these flames leaping.

She knows they feed us,
    that is why she comes,
She never fails us.
    Her name is Joy;
she was not always old.

    for the Lenfesteys and their fires

For Kilian at Ninety

In a glade in the summer woods,
I see you standing.

Everything humming, fluttering, fragrant.

How did you come to be here?
You walked, of course,

as you walk everywhere.

I can imagine nothing that you need to do
after the miles, the years.

save to belong on this holy ground,

all distances, all that was ever beyond,
now gathered within,

your flesh a lamp through which
the spacious spirit, pure being,

shines.

for Kilian McDonnell OSB

Midnight

All the London lives I never led:
meeting an old friend of Dad's

at the pub, by chance, hearing
a story about Dad, how Dad . . .

no, no, that never happened.

Or there's my brother on the couch
below, wind battering his house;

something wakes me, and I know
he's cold; I find him there, TV hissing.

cover him with the blanket that's
fallen to the floor, then climb back up

to my own bed in America.

Emergency Room, Mount Sinai, New York City

they are bombing the city,
    wave upon wave of them,
night after night,
    and so we are huddled
below together, trying to sleep,
    mattresses, bodies everywhere

one man stays awake, sitting up,
    wearing a creased raincoat,
sketching in a small book;
    naked, his mother lies near him,
a gigantic big-breasted woman,
    a huge symmetrical hole in her belly

it is impossible down here, a hothouse,
    but we hear the rattling sounds,
harsher than thunder, so we are staying
    till the wars are ended
till the trees begin to leaf out again
    along the avenues,

till the pale man is young no more
    the cold poles stand restored,
the glaciers, the ice caps
    once again gleaming
like the flesh of prophets,
    and the immense mother mended

    for Mary my daughter,
    Mary my sister

For George McGovern

I was sad to see his belly break up into stars,
to hear the wind under his eyes,
so many rivers streaming out of his face.

I rode out into the foothills looking for him.
I passed sagebrush grievers silently scraping the soil;
I saw the dry soil of stars in the air.

There were too many stories
spread across the sky for me
to be able to tell one from the other,

though sometimes I can still chop away
at the sky or, being human, pan
for even a little gleam of story.

I didn't want anyone to know the miles on me;
I'd rather they thought the stains were wounds,
not rust (rust itself being a kind of wound).

Riding brought back the old times, when waves
of hair once roared across our heads
(you could hear the ocean in our brains).

Now throw me off, old lion, let your mane
be strewn about the sun to light us
anywhere we may yet dare to wander.

October 21, 2012
Wyoming

The Old Happiness

bring back the old happiness
you remember the one

no inner organs laboring
no struggling of the years to come

at yesterday's service for a man
who ended his life, then lingered

the best moment not the kindly
sprightly silver pastor

but the trio of grandchildren
doing a Beatles number, swaying,

pretty much on key and warbling away
in the dialect of the old happiness

Melody

Blind, Melody is brought to your door.
She must be with you for a while;
and tell no one of this guest you hold.

You will know when she must leave
when you yourself can see no longer,
and only with her gone can you begin

the singing which was once against
your will, your power, your dream,
but is now your meaning.

"wanted to be an artist"

wanted to be a fireman
wanted to be a nurse
wanted to be a dancer

hold that flame steady within your hands
        if a wind comes, turn
to where there's no fear for the flame,
        the flame's survival

live as you can with these long shadows
        if you fall into the surrounding reservoirs,
swim as imperceptibly as you can
        over the dark water

wanted to be leaves
wanted to be waves, wings, warm feathers
wanted to be what stays shimmering on the canvas

after the brushes have moved on

for the children and parents of Newtown
12/22/12

For the Wedding of Mary and Marc

On this day of belonging,
   when all longings come home,
when nothing is given away
   only received, received,
we open our hearts to your love.
   We are your sunflowers,
turned toward you.

How should we not be amazed
   at who our children become,
hearts beating faster to see
   such loyalty,
such beauty of being,
   and if we have one wish for them,
it would be:
      love your life

And those who were here before us,
   the invisible company,
if we could imagine
   what *their* prayer might be
for this beloved daughter,
   for this dear new son,
let us guess it could echo our own:
      love your life

Dreams be with you,
    visions be real for you,
harmony of light within you
    as you step into the dance,
of your years of being together,
    today, under this ripe September sun,
so radiantly, so hopefully begun:
        love your life
        love your life
        love your life